STUDY GUIDE

A Six-Session Video-Based Study for Small Groups

YOU MAKE ME CRAZY

SURVIVING RELATIONSHIPS
GOD'S WAY

You Make Me Crazy
Surviving Relationships God's Way

Small Group Study Guide, Edition 1.0

 PastorRick.com

Published by PastorRick.com
23182 Arroyo Vista
Rancho Santa Margarita CA 92688
PastorRick.com

Scripture quotations noted LB are from The Living Bible. Copyright © 1971. Used by permission of Tyndale House Publishers, Wheaton, IL 60189. All rights reserved.

Scripture quotations noted NLT are from the Holy Bible, New Living Translation, copyright © 1996, 2004, 2007 by Tyndale House Foundation. Used by permission of Tyndale House Publishers, Inc., Carol Stream, Illinois 60188. All rights reserved.

Scripture quotations noted NCV are from the New Century Version®. Copyright © 2005 by Thomas Nelson, Inc. Used by permission. All rights reserved.

Scripture quotations noted TEV are from Today's English Version. New Testament, copyright © 1966; Old Testament, copyright © 1976 by American Bible Society. Used by permission. All rights reserved.

Scripture quotations noted NIV are from THE HOLY BIBLE, NEW INTERNATIONAL VERSION®, NIV® Copyright © 1973, 1978, 1984, 2011 by Biblica, Inc.® Used by permission. All rights reserved worldwide.

Scripture quotations noted MSG are from The Message. Copyright © 1993, 1994, 1995, 1996, 2000, 2001, 2002. Used by permission of NavPress Publishing Group.

Scripture quoations noted CEV are from The Contemporary English Version. Copyright © 1991, 1992, 1995 by American Bible Society. Used by permission.

Scripture quotations noted GW are from GOD'S WORD®, © 1995 God's Word to the Nations. Used by permission of Baker Publishing Group.

Scripture quotations noted NKJV are from the New King James Version®. Copyright © 1982 by Thomas Nelson, Inc. Used by permission. All rights reserved.

Scripture quotations noted NJB are from The New Jerusalem Bible, copyright © 1985 by Darton, Longman & Todd, Ltd. and Doubleday, a division of Random House, Inc. Reprinted by Permission.

Scripture quotations noted PH are from J. B. Phillips, "The New Testament in Modern English", 1962 edition, published by HarperCollins.

Scripture quotations noted NRSV are from the New Revised Standard Version Bible, copyright © 1989 the Division of Christian Education of the National Council of the Churches of Christ in the United States of America. Used by permission. All rights reserved.

ISBN: 978-1-4228-0251-9

Printed in the United States of America

TABLE OF CONTENTS

UNDERSTANDING YOUR STUDY GUIDE

Here is a brief explanation of the features of this study guide.

CHECKING IN: You will open each meeting with an opportunity for everyone to check in with each other about how you are doing with the weekly assignments. Accountability is a key to success in this study!

KEY VERSE: Each week you will find a key verse or Scripture passage for your group to read together. If someone in the group has a different translation, ask them to read it aloud so the group can get a bigger picture of the meaning of the passage.

VIDEO LESSON: There is a video lesson for the group to watch together each week. Fill in the blanks in the lesson outlines as you watch the video, and be sure to refer back to these outlines during your discussion time.

DISCOVERY QUESTIONS: Each video segment is complemented by several questions for group discussion. Please don't feel pressured to discuss every single question. There is no reason to rush through the answers. Give everyone ample opportunity to share their thoughts. If you don't get through all of the discussion questions, that's okay.

PUTTING IT INTO PRACTICE: This is where the rubber meets the road. We don't want to be just hearers of the Word. We also need to be doers of the Word (James 1:22). These assignments are application exercises that will help you put into practice the truths you have discussed in the lesson.

PRAYER DIRECTION: At the end of each session you will find suggestions for your group prayer time. Praying together is one of the greatest privileges of small group life. Please don't take it for granted.

A Tip for the Host

The study guide material is meant to be your servant, not your master. The point is not to race through the sessions; the point is to take time to let God work in your lives. Nor is it necessary to "go around the circle" before you move on to the next question. Give people the freedom to speak, but don't insist on it. Your group will enjoy deeper, more open sharing and discussion if people don't feel pressured to speak up.

HOW TO USE THIS VIDEO CURRICULUM

Follow these simple steps for a successful small group meeting:

- Open your group meeting by using the **Checking In** section of your study guide.

- Watch the video lesson together and follow along in the outlines in this study guide. Each video lesson is about fifteen minutes long.

- Complete the rest of the discussion materials for each session. Be sure to review the **Putting It Into Practice** section and commit to fulfilling any action steps before your next session.

- Close your time together by following the **Prayer Direction** suggestions.

SESSION 1

HOW TO BE WISE IN RELATIONSHIPS

CHECKING IN

What are you hoping to get out of this study?

KEY VERSE

Love forgets mistakes; nagging about them parts the best of friends.
Proverbs 17:9 LB

HOW TO BE WISE IN RELATIONSHIPS

If you are wise and understand God's ways, you'll live a life of steady goodness so that only good deeds pour forth. And if you don't brag about the good you do, then you will be truly wise! But if you are bitterly jealous and there is selfish ambition in your hearts, don't brag about being wise. That is the worst kind of lie. For jealousy and selfishness are not God's kind of wisdom. [These] are earthly, unspiritual, and motivated by the Devil. For wherever there is jealousy and selfish ambition, there you will find disorder and every kind of evil. The kind of wisdom that comes from heaven is first of all pure. It is also peace loving, gentle at all times, willing to yield to others. It is full of mercy and good deeds. It shows no partiality and is always sincere. Those who are peacemakers plant seeds of peace and reap a harvest of goodness.
James 3:13-18 NLT

1. Wisdom that comes from heaven is _____.
_____

All relationships are built on trust. All trust is built on truth.

You must stop telling lies. Tell each other the truth, because we all belong to each other in the same body.
Ephesians 4:25 NCV

- **If I want to be wise in my relationships...I won't** _____.

God grants a treasure of good sense to the godly. He is their shield, protecting those who walk with integrity.
Proverbs 2:7 NLT

2. Wisdom is _____.

- **If I want to be wise in my relationships...I won't** _____.

Any fool can start arguments: the honorable thing is to stay out of them.
Proverbs 20:3 TEV

A wise man controls his temper. He knows that anger causes mistakes.
Proverbs 14:29 LB

3. Wisdom is _____.

Let everybody see that you are considerate in all you do.
Philippians 4:5 NLT

Hurt people always hurt people. So look beyond their words to their feelings.

We must be considerate of the doubts and fears of others ..Let's please the other person, not ourselves, in doing what's good for him and build him up.
Romans 15:2 LB

Feelings are neither right nor wrong. They're just there.

- **If I want to be wise in my relationships...I won't** _____.

Kind words bring life, but cruel words crush your spirit.
Proverbs 15:4 TEV

4. Wisdom is willing to _____ to others.

- **If I want to be wise in my relationships...I won't _____.**

Intelligent people are always open to new ideas In fact, they look for them.
Proverbs 18:15 LB

5. Wisdom is full of _____.

- **If I want to be wise in my relationships...I won't _____.**

Love forgets mistakes; nagging about them parts the best of friends.
Proverbs 17:9 LB

6. Wisdom is _____ and always _____.

- **If I want to be wise in my relationships...I won't _____.**

Respect for the Lord is the beginning of wisdom.
Psalm 111:10

Discovery Questions

1. In James 3:17 we learn that wisdom is:

    -   Pure
    -   Peace loving
    -   Gentle
    -   Willing to yield
    -   Full of mercy and good deeds
    -   Impartial and sincere

    Who are the people in your life that you go to for wisdom? Which of these qualities do they display that allow you to trust their wisdom and advice?

2. James 3:14 describes the characteristics that keep us from true wisdom as:

    -   Bitter Jealousy
    -   Selfish Ambition

    Pastor Rick describes these obstacles to wisdom as:

    -   Compromising Integrity
    -   Antagonizing Anger
    -   Minimizing Feelings
    -   Criticizing Suggestions
    -   Emphasizing Mistakes
    -   Disguising Intentions

Have you ever encountered one of these obstacles in your relationships? How did it affect your relationship?

Putting It Into Practice

Review the verses from this lesson and select one to memorize and meditate on this week. Share your chosen verse with the group. What practical steps can you take this week to put that verse into practice? How would it impact your relationships if you put these principles into practice? What changes might you expect to see?

Prayer Direction

As you begin your time of prayer, spend some time thanking God for His generous wisdom.

If you need wisdom, ask our generous God, and he will give it to you.
James 1:5 NLT

Ask God for strength in each of the areas that you have committed to growing in wisdom. Pray for those in your group who are facing significant struggles in their relationships.

SESSION 2

WHO'S PUSHING YOUR BUTTONS?

CHECKING IN

When it comes to relational conflict, are you a skunk or a turtle? Skunks let everybody know about it. Turtles withdraw and keep it to themselves.

KEY VERSE

The fruit of the Spirit is love, joy, peace, patience, kindness, goodness, faithfulness, gentleness, and self-control.
Galatians 5:22-23 NIV

WHO'S PUSHING YOUR BUTTONS?

If you cannot control your anger, you are as helpless as a city without walls, open to attack.
Proverbs 25:28 TEV

A fool is quick-tempered, but a wise person stays calm when insulted.
Proverbs 12:16 NLT

It is better to be patient than powerful; it is better to have self-control than to conquer a city.
Proverbs 16:32 NLT

FOUR CATEGORIES OF ANGER

The _____: they let you have it

The _____: they clam up

Every time you swallow your anger, your stomach keeps score. If you don't talk it out, you're going to take it out on your body.

The _____: they throw pity parties

The _____: they don't get mad, they get even

HOW TO DISARM ANGER

Calculate the _____ of anger.

An angry person causes trouble; a person with a quick temper sins a lot.
Proverbs 29:22 NCV

Hot tempers cause arguments.
Proverbs 15:18a TEV

Anger causes mistakes.
Proverbs 14:29b LB

People with a hot temper do foolish things.
Proverbs 14:17 TEV

Those who control their anger have great understanding, those with a hasty temper make mistakes.
Proverbs 14:29 NLT

Look past their words to _____.

A man's wisdom gives him patience; it is to his glory to overlook an offense.
Proverbs 19:11 NIV

Think before _____.

Anger control is largely a matter of mouth control. Put your mind in gear before you put your mouth in gear.

Sensible people always think before they act.
Proverbs 13:16a TEV

A fool gives full vent to his anger, but a wise person quietly holds it back.
Proverbs 29:11 NLT

Three Causes of Anger:

_____

_____

_____

A gentle answer quiets anger, but a harsh one stirs it up.
Proverbs 15:1 TEV

A wise person uses few words; a person with understanding is even-tempered.
Proverbs 17:27 NLT

Lord, help me control my tongue; help me be careful about what I say.
Psalm 141:3 NCV

The heart of the problem is a problem of the heart. Pressure always reveals what's inside of you.

The fruit of the Spirit is love, joy, peace, patience, kindness, goodness, faithfulness, gentleness, and self-control

Galatians 5:22-23 NIV

Ask God _____.

Base _____ **in Jesus.**

"Grow up. You're kingdom subjects. Now live like it. Live out your God-created identity. Live generously and graciously toward others, the way God lives toward you."

Matthew 5:48 MSG

Jesus can heal your hurting heart with his love. Jesus can replace your frustrated heart with his peace. Jesus can replace your insecure heart with his power.

Discovery Questions

1. Look at the Four Categories of Anger. Which type of person is the most difficult for you to deal with? How do you typically respond to the Machine Gun, Mute, Martyr, and Manipulator?

2. Take an honest inventory of your own anger. Of the Four Categories, which do you most identify with?

3. How has your expression of anger affected your relationships? Have you ever lost anything by losing your temper?

4. Pastor Rick gave us five instructions for disarming anger. Which is the most challenging for you?

Putting It Into Practice

Paul describes the fruit of life in the Spirit as love, joy, peace, patience, kindness, goodness, faithfulness, gentleness, and self-control (Galatians 5:22-23). Which of these qualities would you like to see more of in your own life? How can these qualities help you deal with your anger?

Prayer Direction

Spend some time in silence asking God to reveal areas of hidden or masked anger in your life. Pray specifically for Jesus to:

- Heal your hurting heart with his love
- Replace your frustrated heart with his peace
- Replace your insecure heart with his power

Pray for those in your group who are struggling to manage their anger. Ask God to bring a Spirit of peace and healing.

SESSION

3

HOW TO
RESOLVE CONFLICT

CHECKING IN

Share with the group how the qualities you worked on since your last meeting have helped you deal with your anger.

KEY VERSE

Be quick to listen, slow to speak, and slow to get angry.
James 1:19 NLT

HOW TO RESOLVE CONFLICT

Never pay back evil for evil to anyone. As much as possible, as far as it depends on you, live in peace with everyone.
Romans 12:17-18 NLT

SEVEN STEPS FOR RESOLVING CONFLICT

1. Take the _____.

"If you're standing before the altar in the temple and you suddenly remember that somebody has something against you, leave your offering there beside the altar. Go at once and first be reconciled to that person. Then come and offer your gift to God."
Matthew 5:23-24 NLT

Four things you must do in setting up the meeting:

- **Choose the _____.**

- **Choose the _____.**

- **_____ before the meeting.**

- **Come with a _____.**

2. Confess my part of the _____.

"Why do you notice the little piece of dust in your friend's eye, but you don't notice the big piece of wood in your own eye?. . . First, take the wood out of your own eye. Then you will see clearly to take the dust out of your friend's eye."
Matthew 7:3-5 NCV

3. Listen for the _____.

Be quick to listen, slow to speak, and slow to get angry.
James 1:19 NLT

We must be considerate of the doubts and the fears of others.
Romans 15:2 NLT

4. Consider their _____.

Each of you should look not only to your own interests, but also to the interests of others. Your attitude should be the same as that of Christ Jesus.
Philippians 2:4-5 NIV

God, you notice everything I do and everywhere I go.
Psalm 139:3 CEV

5. Tell the truth tactfully.

Reckless words pierce like a sword, but the tongue of the wise brings healing.
Proverbs 12:18 NIV

You never get your point across by being cross. You are never persuasive when you are abrasive.

Do not use harmful words, but only helpful words, the kind that build up and provide what is needed.
Ephesians 4:29 TEV

6. Fix the _____, not the _____.

You must rid yourself of all such things as these: anger, rage, malice, slander, and filthy language from your lips.
Colossians 3:8 NIV

When you belittle someone you are showing how tiny your heart is. Only little people belittle people. Great people make people feel great.

Let us stop passing judgment on one another. Instead, make up your mind not to put any stumbling block or obstacle in your brother's way.
Romans 14:13 NIV

7. Focus on _____, not _____.

If you learn to disagree without being disagreeable, that's called wisdom. If you learn that you can have unity without uniformity, that's called wisdom. If you learn to walk hand in hand without having to see eye to eye, that's called wisdom.

"Blessed are the peacemakers."
Matthew 5:9a NIV

It's always more rewarding to _____ the conflict than to _____ the relationship.

You can't make peace with other people until you make peace with God.

There is only one God and one Mediator who can reconcile God and people. He is Jesus Christ.
1 Timothy 2:5 NLT

Discovery Questions

1. Jesus encourages us to initiate conflict resolution right away (Matthew 5:24.) Is there currently an unresolved conflict in your life? What is keeping you from taking the initiative to resolve it?

2. Look back at the 7 steps for resolving conflict. Which of these is the most difficult step for you to take?

3. What doubts and fears in yourself do you wish others would be mindful of when approaching you about a conflict? How does identifying these help you to consider the perspective of others?

4. What would it look like for you to seek reconciliation as opposed to resolution in your current conflicts? What would you have to surrender to make that possible?

Putting It Into Practice

Make plans to take the initiative right now. Who do you need to text, call or email when you get home? When is the right time to meet? Where is the right place? What do you need to surrender in order to come with a positive attitude?

Prayer Direction

Ask your group to hold you accountable to initiating conflict resolution. Pray for one another, for the humility and flexibility needed to seek reconciliation rather than resolution. Commit to praying for each other at the times of your scheduled meetings.

SESSION 4

BREAKING FREE FROM ABUSE

CHECKING IN

You may have experienced the difficulty of conflict resolution since your last meeting. If you feel comfortable, share your experience with your group.

KEY VERSE

"The truth will set you free."
John 8:32 NIV

BREAKING FREE FROM ABUSE

SEVEN STEPS TO FREEDOM

1. Don't keep it a _____.

If you're afraid to talk about it, it's already dominating and controlling your life.

"The truth will set you free."
John 8:32 NIV

2. Name the _____.

Eight kinds of emotional abuse:

• _____

My enemies taunt me day after day. They mock and curse me.
Psalm 102:8 NLT

• _____

They tell lies about me and they threaten me.
Psalm 109:20 LB

- _____

They make fun of me and they ridicule me.
Psalm 22:7

- _____

I've been insulted, put to shame and humiliated.
Psalm 69:19 GW

- _____

They jeer, using words to kill; they bully their way with words.
Psalm 73:8 MSG

- _____

They pushed hard to make me fall.
Psalm 118:13 GW

- _____

They spread rumors about me, and conspire against me.
Psalm 31:13 NLT

- _____

They mock me with the worst kind of profanity, and snarl at me.
Psalm 35:16

3. Don't _____ it, don't _____ it.

Don't be fooled by those who try to excuse these sins, for the anger of God comes upon all those who disobey him.
Ephesians 5:6 NLT

4. Help them to a _____ if necessary.

Carry each other's burdens, and in this way you will fulfill the law of Christ.
Galatians 6:2 NIV

5. Don't _____ an abuser by yourself.

By yourself you're unprotected. With a friend you can face the worst. Can you get a third? A three-stranded rope isn't easily snapped.
Ecclesiastes 4:12 MSG

Let him who thinks he stands take heed lest he fall

1 Corinthians 10:12 NKJV

...restore him gently.

Galatians 6:1 NIV

6. Begin the _____.

Job, put your heart right. Reach out to God. Put away evil and wrong from your home. Then face the world again, firm and courageous. Then all your troubles will fade from your memory, like floods that are past and remembered no more. Your life will be brighter than the sunshine at noon, and life's darkest hours will shine like the dawn.

Job 11:13-17 TEV

7. Let God _____.

Never repay one wrong with another, or one abusive word with another, instead, repay with a blessing. That is what you are called to do, so that you inherit a blessing.

1 Peter 3:9 NJB

Christ never verbally abused those who verbally abused him. When he suffered, he didn't make any threats but left everything to the one who judges fairly.

1 Peter 2:23 GW

Discovery Questions

1. Pastor Rick gave us seven steps to break free from abuse. Which of these is the most challenging for you?

2. As we consider the 8 types of emotional abuse, it becomes clear that we all have experience with abuse. Where do you find yourself minimizing or rationalizing the abuse that has been done to you? Where do you find yourself minimizing or rationalizing the abuse you have inflicted on others?

Putting It Into Practice

Breaking free from abuse isn't a one-time decision—no matter how big or small the abuse is perceived to be. It's a journey. Pastor Rick shared that the first step to breaking free from abuse is to not keep it a secret. Who is a trusted person in your life that you can share your experiences with? Reach out to that person and begin the conversation and your journey to healing.

Prayer Direction

There is healing available for both the abused and the abuser. Ask God to give you the strength and courage to end the cycle of abuse.

SESSION 5

ESCAPING THE PEOPLE-PLEASER TRAP

CHECKING IN

Last session, we talked about breaking free from abuse. Open your time today in a time of prayer, asking God to continue to strengthen you as you break the cycles of abuse in your lives.

KEY VERSE

It is a dangerous trap to be concerned with what others think of you, but if you trust the Lord, you are safe.
Proverbs 29:25 TEV

ESCAPING THE PEOPLE-PLEASER TRAP

"When you know the truth, the truth will set you free."
John 8:32

SIX ANTIDOTES TO APPROVAL ADDICTION

1. Even God _____ **everybody.**

"Woe to you when all men speak well of you."
Luke 6:26 NKJV

2. I don't need _____ **to be happy!**

"Your approval or disapproval means nothing to me."
John 5:41 LB

The bigger God is in your life, the smaller people are in your life. The bigger you make people in your life, the smaller God is.

Even if my father and mother abandon me, the Lord will hold me close.
Psalm 27:10 NLT

3. What seems so important now is _____
_____.

The world and everything in it that people desire is passing away; but those who do the will of God live forever.
1 John 2:17 TEV

Short-term thinking leads to people pleasing, but an eternal perspective leads to freedom.

"The things that are [highly valued] by people are worth nothing in God's sight."
Luke 16:15b TEV

4. I only have to please _____.

"I don't try to please myself, but I [only] please the One who sent me."
John 5:30 NCV

People-pleasing is a form of idolatry, because their opinion matters more than God's opinion. At that point, you have another god in your life.

I'm not trying to be a people pleaser! No, I'm trying to please God. If I was still trying to please people, I would not be Christ's servant.

Galatians 1:10 NLT

5. One day I'll give _____ of my life.

Yes, each of us will give a personal account to God.

Romans 14:12 NLT

"If anyone is ashamed of me and my words, the Son of Man will be ashamed of him when he comes in his glory and in the glory of the Father and of the holy angels."

Luke 9:26 NIV

Will Jesus be ashamed of you because you were ashamed of him?

6. God _____ to be me.

When you get to heaven, God is not going to ask, "Why weren't you more like your brother or father or mother?" He's going to ask, "Did you become who I made you to be? Did you fulfill the purpose I created you for?"

Don't let the world squeeze you into its own mould, but let God re-mould your minds from within, so that you may prove in practice that the plan of God for you is good...

Romans 12:2 PH

Discovery Questions

1. Consider the different relationships in your life:

    *   Family
    *   Work
    *   Friends

    Where do you find yourself falling prey to the people-pleaser trap?

2. Pastor Rick shared 6 truths to combat approval addiction. Which of these truths is the most encouraging to you?

3. If you adopted these truths, how would your life be different? What are some of the specific things you would say "no" to? What are the things you would say "yes" to?

Putting It Into Practice

Look through the Bible verses from this lesson. Which one can you hold on to when faced with the temptation to please others? What is one realistic step you can take this week to avoid the people-pleasing trap?

Prayer Direction

Spend some time thanking God for the unique way He created you. Ask God for the courage to live for Him alone.

KEEPING THE CRAZY-MAKERS FROM MAKING YOU CRAZY

CHECKING IN

Share with the group your experience of taking a first step in avoiding the people-pleasing trap.

KEY VERSE

Do not be overcome by evil, but overcome evil with good.
Romans 12:21 NIV

KEEPING THE CRAZY-MAKERS FROM MAKING YOU CRAZY

SIX TYPES OF CRAZY-MAKERS

- _____

- _____

- _____

- _____

- _____

- _____

HOW TO DEAL WITH DIFFICULT PEOPLE

Refuse to be _____.

Emotional and spiritual maturity is largely determined by how you treat those who mistreat you.

When a fool is annoyed he quickly lets it be known [Wise] people will ignore an insult.
Proverbs 12:16 TEV

A man's wisdom gives him patience; it is to his glory to overlook an offense.
Proverbs 19:11 NIV

Love overlooks the wrongs that others do.
Proverbs 10:12b CEV

Don't wait for _____ **to forgive them.**

"Father, forgive them, for they do not know what they are doing."
Luke 23:34 NIV

You must make allowance for each other's faults and forgive the person who offends you. Remember, the Lord forgave you, so you must forgive others.
Colossians 3:13 NLT

"Blessed are the merciful for they will receive mercy."
Matthew 5:7 NRSV

Refuse to _____ about them.

Disregarding other people's faults preserves love; but gossiping about them separates close friends.
Proverbs 17:9 NLT

Do not do wrong to repay a wrong, and do not insult to repay an insult. But repay with a blessing, because you yourselves were called to do this so that you might receive a blessing.
1 Peter 3:9 NCV

Refuse to _____ their game.

Just as charcoal and wood keep a fire going, a quarrelsome person keeps an argument going.
Proverbs 26:21 NCV

Throw out the mocker, and you'll be rid of tension, fighting and quarrels.
Proverbs 22:10 LB

Refuse to _____.

Forgiveness and trust are two different things. Forgiveness is instant. Trust must be earned.

You let people make slaves of you and cheat you and steal from you. Why, you even let them strut around and slap you in the face.
2 Corinthians 11:20 NCV

You even put up with anyone who enslaves you or exploits you or takes advantage of you or pushes himself forward or slaps you in the face.
2 Corinthians 11:20 NIV

We have freedom now, because Christ made us free. So stand strong. Do not change and go back into the slavery of the law.
Galatians 5:1 NCV

Always take the _____.

Ask God to bless those who persecute you – yes, ask him to bless, not to curse.
Romans 12:14 TEV

Do not be overcome by evil, but overcome evil with good.
Romans 12:21 NIV

When a man's ways are pleasing to the Lord, he makes even his enemies live at peace with him.
Proverbs 16:7 NIV

Discovery Questions

1. Which of the six types of crazy-makers do you find yourself dealing with most often?

2. As Pastor Rick said, our spiritual and emotional maturity is determined by our response to those who misunderstand and mistreat us. Look at the 6 principles for dealing with difficult people. Where might God be challenging you to grow in maturity?

3. Why is it difficult for people to "take the high ground?" How can you take the high ground the next time you encounter a crazy-maker in your life?

Putting It Into Practice

To deal with the crazy-makers in our lives, we must rely on God's strength. What Bible verse from this week's lesson can you look to for strength as you deal with the difficult people in your life?

Prayer Direction

Thank God for the relationships in your life—even the crazy-making ones! Ask God to help you extend forgiveness to anyone you've been holding a grudge against.

SMALL GROUP RESOURCES

HELPS FOR HOSTS

TOP TEN IDEAS FOR NEW HOSTS

CONGRATULATIONS! As the host of your small group, you have responded to the call to help shepherd Jesus' flock. Few other tasks in the family of God surpass the contribution you will be making. As you prepare to facilitate your group, whether it is one session or the entire series, here are a few thoughts to keep in mind.

Remember you are not alone. God knows everything about you, and He knew you would be asked to facilitate your group. Even though you may not feel ready, this is common for all good hosts. God promises, *"I will never leave you; I will never abandon you"* (Hebrews 13:5 TEV). Whether you are facilitating for one evening, several weeks, or a lifetime, you will be blessed as you serve.

1. **DON'T TRY TO DO IT ALONE.** Pray right now for God to help you build a healthy team. If you can enlist a co-host to help you shepherd the group, you will find your experience much richer. This is your chance to involve as many people as you can in building a healthy group. All you have to do is ask people to help. You'll be surprised at the response.

2. **BE FRIENDLY AND BE YOURSELF.** God wants to use your unique gifts and temperament. Be sure to greet people at the door with a big smile . . . this can set the mood for the whole gathering. Remember, they are taking as big a step to show up at your house as you are to host a small group! Don't try to do things exactly like another host; do them in a way that fits you. Admit when you don't have an answer and apologize when you make a mistake. Your group will love you for it and you'll sleep better at night.

3. **PREPARE FOR YOUR MEETING AHEAD OF TIME.** Review the session and write down your responses to each question. Pay special attention to the Putting It Into Practice exercises that ask group members to do something other than engage in discussion. These exercises will help your group live what the Bible teaches, not just talk about it.

4. **PRAY FOR YOUR GROUP MEMBERS BY NAME.** Before you begin your session, take a few moments and pray for each member by name. You may want to review the Small Group Prayer and Praise Report at least once a week. Ask God to use your time together to touch the heart of each person in your group. Expect God to lead you to whomever He wants you to encourage or challenge in a special way. If you listen, God will surely lead.

5. **WHEN YOU ASK A QUESTION, BE PATIENT.** Someone will eventually respond. Sometimes people need a moment or two of silence to think about the question. If silence doesn't bother you, it won't bother anyone else. After someone responds, affirm the response with a simple "thanks" or "great answer." Then ask, "How about somebody else?" or "Would someone who hasn't shared like to add anything?" Be sensitive to new people or reluctant members who aren't ready to say, pray, or do anything. If you give them a safe setting, they will blossom over time. If someone in your group is a wallflower who sits silently through every session, consider talking to them privately and encouraging them to participate. Let them know how important they are to you—that they are loved and appreciated, and that the group would value their input. Remember, still water often runs deep.

6. **PROVIDE TRANSITIONS BETWEEN QUESTIONS.** Ask if anyone would like to read the paragraph or Bible passage. Don't call on anyone, but ask for a volunteer, and then be patient until someone begins. Be sure to thank the person who reads aloud.

7. **BREAK INTO SMALLER GROUPS OCCASIONALLY.** With a greater opportunity to talk in a small circle, people will connect more with the study, apply more quickly what they're learning, and ultimately get more out of their small group experience. A small circle also encourages a quiet person to participate and tends to minimize the effects of a more vocal or dominant member.

8. **SMALL CIRCLES ARE ALSO HELPFUL DURING PRAYER TIME.** People who are unaccustomed to praying aloud will feel more comfortable trying it with just two or three others. Also, prayer requests won't take as much time, so circles will have more time to actually pray. When you gather back with the whole group, you can have one person from each circle briefly update everyone on the prayer requests from their subgroups. The other great aspect of subgrouping is that it fosters leadership development. As you ask people in the group to facilitate discussion or to lead a prayer circle, it gives them a small leadership step that can build their confidence.

9. **ROTATE FACILITATORS OCCASIONALLY.** You may be perfectly capable of hosting each time, but you will help others grow in their faith and gifts if you give them opportunities to host the group.

10. **ONE FINAL CHALLENGE (FOR NEW OR FIRST-TIME HOSTS).** Before your first opportunity to lead, look up each of the six passages listed below. Read each one as a devotional exercise to help prepare you with a shepherd's heart. Trust us on this one. If you do this, you will be more than ready for your first meeting.

MATTHEW 9:36–38 (NIV)

[36]When Jesus saw the crowds, he had compassion on them, because they were harassed and helpless, like sheep without a shepherd.

[37]Then he said to his disciples, "The harvest is plentiful but the workers are few. [38]Ask the Lord of the harvest, therefore, to send out workers into his harvest field."

JOHN 10:14–15 (NIV)

[14]I am the good shepherd; I know my sheep and my sheep know me—[15]just as the Father knows me and I know the Father—and I lay down my life for the sheep.

1 PETER 5:2–4 (NIV)

[2]Be shepherds of God's flock that is under your care, serving as overseers—not because you must, but because you are willing, as God wants you to be; [3]not greedy for money, but eager to serve; not lording it over those entrusted to you, but being examples to the flock. [4]And when the Chief Shepherd appears, you will receive the crown of glory that will never fade away.

PHILIPPIANS 2:1–5 (NIV)

[1]If you have any encouragement from being united with Christ, if any comfort from his love, if any fellowship with the Spirit, if any tenderness and compassion, [2]then make my joy complete by being like-minded, having the same love, being one in spirit and purpose. [3]Do nothing out of selfish ambition or vain conceit, but in humility consider others better than yourselves. [4]Each of you should look not only to your own interests, but also to the interests of others. [5]Your attitude should be the same as that of Jesus Christ.

HEBREWS 10:23–25 (NIV)

23Let us hold unswervingly to the hope we profess, for he who promised is faithful. 24And let us consider how we may spur one another on toward love and good deeds. 25Let us not give up meeting together, as some are in the habit of doing, but let us encourage one another—and all the more as you see the Day approaching.

1 THESSALONIANS 2:7–8, 11–12 (NIV)

7...but we were gentle among you, like a mother caring for her little children. 8We loved you so much that we were delighted to share with you not only the gospel of God but our lives as well, because you had become so dear to us.... 11For you know that we dealt with each of you as a father deals with his own children, 12encouraging, comforting and urging you to live lives worthy of God, who calls you into his kingdom and glory.

FREQUENTLY ASKED QUESTIONS

How long will this group meet?

This study is six sessions long. We encourage your group to add a seventh session for a celebration. In your final session, each group member may decide if he or she desires to continue on for another study. At that time you may also want to do some informal evaluation, discuss your group guidelines, and decide which study you want to do next. We recommend you visit our website at www.saddlebackresources.com for more video-based small group studies.

Who is the host?

The host is the person who coordinates and facilitates your group meetings. In addition to a host, we encourage you to select one or more group members to lead your group discussions. Several other responsibilities can be rotated, including refreshments, prayer requests, worship, or keeping up with those who miss a meeting. Shared ownership in the group helps everybody grow.

Where do we find new group members?

Recruiting new members can be a challenge for groups, especially new groups with just a few people, or existing groups that lose a few people along the way. We encourage you to use the Circles of Life diagram on page 48 of this study guide to brainstorm a list of people from your workplace, church, school, neighborhood, family, and so on. Then pray for the people on each member's list. Allow each member to invite several people from their list. Some groups fear that newcomers will interrupt the intimacy that members have built over time. However, groups that welcome newcomers generally gain strength with the infusion of new blood. Remember, the next person you add just might become a friend for eternity. Logistically, groups find different ways to add members. Some groups remain permanently open, while others choose to open periodically, such as at the beginning or end of a study. If your group becomes too large for easy, face-to-face conversations, you can subgroup, forming a second discussion group in another room.

How do we handle the childcare needs in our group?

Childcare needs must be handled very carefully. This is a sensitive issue. We suggest you seek creative solutions as a group. One common solution is to have the adults meet in the living room and share the cost of a baby sitter (or two) who can be with the kids in another part of the house.

Another popular option is to have one home for the kids and a second home (close by) for the adults. If desired, the adults could rotate the responsibility of providing a lesson for the kids. This last option is great with school-age kids and can be a huge blessing to families.

CIRCLES OF LIFE

SMALL GROUP CONNECTIONS

Discover Who You Can Connect in Community
Use this chart to help carry out one of the values in the Group Guidelines, to "Welcome Newcomers."

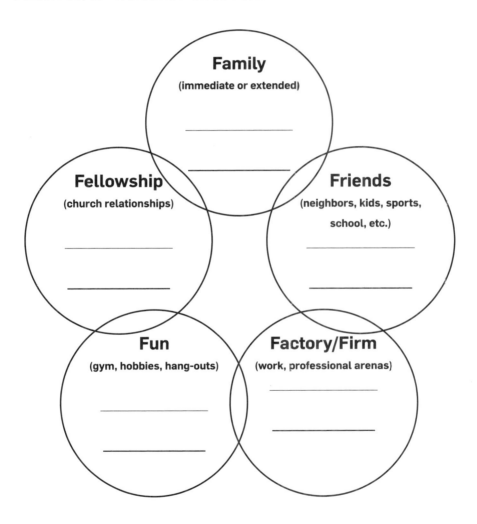

Follow this simple three-step process:

1. List one to two people in each circle.

2. Prayerfully select one person or couple from your list and tell your group about them.

3. Give them a call and invite them to your next meeting. Over fifty percent of those invited to a small group say, "Yes!"

GROUP GUIDELINES

It's a good idea for every group to put words to their shared values, expectations, and commitments. Such guidelines will help you avoid unspoken agendas and unmet expectations. We recommend you discuss your guidelines during Session 1 in order to lay the foundation for a healthy group experience. Feel free to modify anything that does not work for your group.

We agree to the following values:

CLEAR PURPOSE	To grow healthy spiritual lives by building a healthy small group community
GROUP ATTENDANCE	To give priority to the group meeting (call if I am absent or late)
SAFE ENVIRONMENT	To create a safe place where people can be heard and feel loved (no quick answers, snap judgments, or simple fixes)
BE CONFIDENTIAL	To keep anything that is shared strictly confidential and within the group
CONFLICT RESOLUTION	To avoid gossip and to immediately resolve any concerns by following the principles of Matthew 18:15–17
SPIRITUAL HEALTH	To give group members permission to speak into my life and help me live a healthy, balanced spiritual life that is pleasing to God

LIMIT OUR FREEDOM	To limit our freedom by not serving or consuming alcohol during small group meetings or events so as to avoid causing a weaker brother or sister to stumble (1 Corinthians 8:1–13; Romans 14:19–21)
WELCOME NEWCOMERS	To invite friends who might benefit from this study and warmly welcome newcomers
BUILDING RELATIONSHIPS	To get to know the other members of the group and pray for them regularly
OTHER	_____

We have also discussed and agree on the following items:

CHILD CARE   _____

STARTING TIME   _____

ENDING TIME   _____

If you haven't already done so, take a few minutes to fill out the Small Group Calendar on page 54.

SMALL GROUP PRAYER AND PRAISE REPORT

This is a place where you can write each other's requests for prayer. You can also make a note when God answers a prayer. Pray for each other's requests. If you're new to group prayer, it's okay to pray silently or to pray by using just one sentence:

"God, please help _____ to _____ ."

DATE	PERSON	PRAYER REQUEST	PRAISE REPORT

DATE	PERSON	PRAYER REQUEST	PRAISE REPORT

SMALL GROUP CALENDAR

Healthy groups share responsibilities and group ownership. It might take some time for this to develop. Shared ownership ensures that responsibility for the group doesn't fall to one person. Use the calendar to keep track of social events, mission projects, birthdays, or days off. Complete this calendar at your first or second meeting. Planning ahead will increase attendance and shared ownership.

DATE	LESSON	LOCATION	FACILITATOR	SNACK OR MEAL
	Session 1			
	Session 2			
	Session 3			
	Session 4			

DATE	LESSON	LOCATION	FACILITATOR	SNACK OR MEAL
	Session 5			
	Session 6			
	Celebration			

ANSWER KEY

SESSION 1

1. Wisdom that comes from heaven is PURE.
- If I want to be wise in my relationships...I won't COMPROMISE MY INTEGRITY.

2. Wisdom is PEACE LOVING.
- If I want to be wise in my relationships...I won't ANTAGONIZE YOUR ANGER.

3. Wisdom is GENTLE.
- If I want to be wise in my relationships...I won't MINIMIZE YOUR FEELINGS.

4. Wisdom is willing to YIELD to others.
- If I want to be wise in my relationships...I won't CRITICIZE YOUR SUGGESTIONS.

5. Wisdom is full of MERCY and GOOD DEEDS.
- If I want to be wise in my relationships ...I won't EMPHASIZE YOUR MISTAKES.

6. Wisdom is IMPARTIAL and always SINCERE.
- If I want to be wise in my relationships...I won't DISGUISE MY INTENTIONS.

SESSION 2

Four Categories of Anger

The MACHINE GUNS: they let you have it

The MUTES: they clam up

The MARTYRS: they throw pity parties

The MANIPULATORS: they don't get mad, they get even

How to Disarm Anger

Calculate the COST of anger.

Look past their words to THEIR PAIN.

Think before REACTING.

Three Causes of Anger
- HURT
- FRUSTRATION
- FEAR

Ask God FOR HELP.

Base YOUR IDENTITY in Jesus.

SESSION 3

Seven Steps for Resolving Conflict

1. Take the INITIATIVE.

Four things you must do in setting up the meeting:

- Choose the RIGHT TIME.
- Choose the RIGHT PLACE.
- PRAY before the meeting.
- Come with a POSITIVE ATTITUDE.

2. Confess my part of the CONFLICT.

3. Listen for the HURT.

4. Consider their PERSPECTIVE.

5. Tell the truth TACTFULLY.

6. Fix the PROBLEM, not the BLAME.

7. Focus on RECONCILIATION, not RESOLUTION.

It's always more rewarding to RESOLVE the conflict than to DISSOLVE the relationship.

SESSION 4

Seven Steps to Freedom

1. Don't keep it A SECRET.

2. Name the ABUSE.

Eight kinds of Emotional Abuse:

- AGGRAVATION
- INTIMIDATION
- DENIGRATION
- HUMILIATION
- MANIPULATION
- DOMINATION

- DEFAMATION
- CONDEMNATION

3. Don't MINIMIZE it, con't RATIONALIZE it.

4. Help them to a SAFE PLACE if necessary.

5. Don't CONFRONT an abuser by yourself.

6. Begin the HEALING PROCESS.

7. Let God SETTLE THE SCORE.

SESSION 5

Six Antidotes to Approval Addiction

1. Even God CAN'T PLEASE everybody.

2. I don't need ANYONE'S APPROVAL to be happy!

3. What seems so important now is ONLY TEMPORARY.

4. I only have to please ONE PERSON.

5. One day I'll give AN ACCOUNT of my life.

6. God shaped me to be me.

ANSWER KEY

SESSION 6
Six Types of Crazy-Makers
- <u>DEMANDING</u>
- <u>DISAPPROVING</u>
- <u>DEAFENING</u>
- <u>DESTRUCTIVE</u>
- <u>DISCONTENTED</u>
- <u>DEMEANING</u>

How to Deal with Difficult People
Refuse to be <u>OFFENDED</u>.

Don't wait for <u>AN APOLOGY</u> to forgive them.

Refuse to <u>GOSSIP</u> about them.

Refuse to <u>PLAY</u> their game.

Refuse to <u>CAVE IN</u>.

Always take the <u>HIGH GROUND</u>.

KEY VERSES

Session 1
Proverbs 17:9 LB
Love forgets mistakes; nagging about them parts the best of friends.

Session 2
Galatians 5:22-23 NIV
The fruit of the Spirit is love, joy, peace, patience, kindness, goodness, faithfulness, gentleness, and self-control.

Session 3
James 1:19 NLT
Be quick to listen, slow to speak, and slow to get angry.

Session 4
John 8:32 NIV
"The truth will set you free."

Session 5
Proverbs 29:25 TEV
It is a dangerous trap to be concerned with what others think of you, but if you trust the Lord, you are safe.

Session 6
Romans 12:21 NIV
Do not be overcome by evil, but overcome evil with good.

ADDITIONAL NOTES

ADDITIONAL NOTES

ADDITIONAL NOTES

ADDITIONAL NOTES